AF482260

SHORT QUOTES FROM THE KINGS NOTES
FROM THE AUTHORIZED KING JAMES BIBLE

RESURRECTION OF THE DEAD

by Elder Roland John Buras

RoseDog Books

PITTSBURGH, PENNSYLVANIA 15238

The contents of this work, including, but not limited to, the accuracy of events, people, and places depicted; opinions expressed; permission to use previously published materials included; and any advice given or actions advocated are solely the responsibility of the author, who assumes all liability for said work and indemnifies the publisher against any claims stemming from publication of the work.

All Rights Reserved

Copyright © 2023 by Elder Roland John Buras

No part of this book may be reproduced or transmitted, downloaded, distributed, reverse engineered, or stored in or introduced into any information storage and retrieval system, in any form or by any means, including photocopying and recording, whether electronic or mechanical, now known or hereinafter invented without permission in writing from the publisher.

RoseDog Books
585 Alpha Drive
Suite 103
Pittsburgh, PA 15238
Visit our website at www.rosedogbookstore.com

ISBN: 979-8-88683-428-4
eISBN: 979-8-88683-409-3

SHORT QUOTES FROM THE KINGS NOTES
FROM THE AUTHORIZED KING JAMES BIBLE

RESURRECTION OF THE DEAD

To You that do not know me, I introduce Myself, Roland John Buras, From Down the Road Known as R J Buras from Venice Louisiana. My Roots begin there on December 6th, 1949.

Blessed with many talents brought Me to where I am today. Among the most important events in my Life is the one of meeting My Wonderful wife, Charlotte Jean {Carley} Buras. The Second was Meeting The Lord Jesus Christ. And so, our Life continues on with Five Children, A Ministry of Evangelizing, Music, and A Family full of Love.

Thus, my Inspiration to write on this Subject of" The Resurrection Of the Dead". I am not an Authority of the Subject, just a Thinker of the Future. A wonderer of the Faith and a Listener to the Voice of God. A Devoted Husband of One Wife, Father of Five, and A Christian of the Lord Jesus Christ.

CHAPTER 1

"LET US BEGIN"
RESURRECTION OF THE DEAD

The theme of Events at Calvary not only represented The Death, The Burial and Resurrection of Our Lord and Savior Jesus Christ, but is the Pre-example of the event and happening of every Human Body Of a Person that has been Born again, John 3: 5,6,7,

The Event' is Described in the word of God as the First Fruits from the Dead; Jesus Christ being the First fruits of them that Sleep, {The Dead} He has provided this better hope for us. The Bible declares in John 5:39, Search the scriptures for in them ye think ye have eternal life, for they {the Scriptures} are they which do testify of Me, The Lord Jesus Christ. Now I ask you The Reader, is there scripture for the Resurrection of the Natural body? Dead Or Alive, or is the resurrection just for the departed spirit of that natural body. In other words, will your body of Flesh be Resurrected from the Dead? or will your departed spirit have a different body?

The reason I ask these questions, are, to have you diligently look at the scriptures.

In the book of first Corinthians chapter 15 we find a very detailed analysis of this event.

'Quoting' in 1st Corinthians, 15:12, Now if Christ be preached that he rose from the dead, how say some among you that there is no resurrection of the dead? Among some it is still said today there is not a resurrection of the Dead: In Corinthian's Chapter 15 Verse 14 it says, And if Christ

be not risen, then is our Preaching in Vain, and your Faith is also in Vain. And Verse 15 1st Corinthians, Declares, Yea, and we are found False witnesses of God because we have testified of God that he raised up the human body of Jesus Christ:

BODILY CORRUPTION TO INCORRUPTION

So, Continuing with 1st. Corinthian's verse 16; For if the Dead rise not then is Christ not raised: And Verse 17, And if Christ be not raised, your faith is vain; and ye are yet in your sins.

Apostle Paul said in Verse 18; Then they' the Saints, also which are fallen asleep in Christ are Perished. With That Meaning: The Human Body has no Hope. Now Remember, the above scriptures that are quoted pertain to that of a Physical Body, FLESH, not the Spirit.

The Spirit of a person that has died, The Spirit does not suffer the elements of Corruption or perishing, only a Physical, Mortal Body can experience such a Change.

The Apostle Paul Quoted to the Corinthians in Verse 19: If In This Life Only {OUR Present Earthly Life} We have Hope in Christ, And He has not Resurrected from the Dead, Then WE are of All Men Most Miserable; Just Think about that.

However, in the Book of 1st Corinthians 15:20 we read, 'But now is Christ Risen from the Dead and became the first fruits of them that slept, (He Died, He Was Buried, and He Resurrected).

By this act comes, The Resurrection of the Dead' The Bodily Resurrection of Jesus Christ Destroys your Enemy' DEATH, which He destroyed by His Resurrection.

This my Friend is the Main Theme of Calvary, the Death, The Burial and The Resurrection of Jesus Christ. Also, the above defines the Prerequisites for True Christian Identification. We find the First act of The Lord at Calvary was 'Death, 2cd Timothy 2:11. We that may be New to the Gospel or Touched by a witness of these things of Christs, causing us to become sorrowful and to first Repent of our sins, Acts 2:38 and turn away from them, dying out you might say to Sin'

A type of Death, Quote in Romans 6:3 Know ye not, that so many of us that were Baptized into Jesus Christ were Baptized unto his Death? Therefore, we or buried with him by Baptism into Death That like as Christ was Raised up from the dead by the glory of the Father, even so WE also should walk in newness of Life.

Romans 6: Vs. 5, For if we have been planted together in the likeness of his death We shall be also in the Likeness of his Resurrection. So then, once we have repented of our sins and have been Baptized in his Name, and forsaken those sins," we want to be rid and clean of them.

So that which is Dead must be Buried, NOTE* Not all Churches Bury their Dead! Colossians 2:12. Buried with him in Baptism, wherein also you or risen with him through the

Faith of the operation of God, who hath raised him {JESUS CHRIST} from the dead.

The Grave for Burying the dead and their sins comes through a grave of Water, 1st Peter 3:20. Speaking of the days when God was waiting while Noah was preparing the ark wherein few, that is, eight souls were saved by water.

1st Peter 3: Vs. 21

The like figure whereunto Even Baptism doth also now Save us, (Not the putting away the filth of the flesh, But the answer of a Good Conscience toward God,) by the resurrection of Jesus Christ.

Almost Unbelievable, the Significance and the power of the Mystery of Christ, And of Water Baptism. In Acts 8:26 through Verse 39, The Angel of the Lord Instructed Phillip to go South from Jerusalem through Gaza which is Desert, He arose and went and found a man of Ethiopia,

A Eunuch of Great Authority under Candace, Queen of the Ethiopian's who had come to Jerusalem for to Worship, Returning, the eunuch sitting in his Chariot Reading Isaiah the Prophet, The Spirit of the Lord told Phillip to go and join himself to the Chariot, and Phillip ran to him and heard him reading Isaiah the Prophet, and Phillip said, Understandeth what thou Readeth?

And He said how can I except some man should guide me, Then Phillip Opened his mouth and began at the same scripture to speak unto him JESUS, as they went on their way the Eunuch said See here is Water, what doth Hinder me to be Baptized and commanded the Chariot to stand still and He and Phillip went down into the water,

Both Phillip and the Eunuch and He Baptized Him, and when they were come up out of the water' The Spirit caught away Phillip that the Eunuch saw Phillip no more and went on his way rejoicing.

However, the Watery Grave has a dual Nature Spiritually. One, for Burying in the Watery Grave the repented "died to sin" candidate, and Two: for the Spiritual Resurrection of the Candidate raised unto the Newness of life.

Romans 6:4. Remember without the Shedding of Blood" = Death, there is no Remission of Sins, Hebrew 9:22. Only Jesus Christ could play that Role, As A Lamb Led to The Slaughter, Isaiah 53:7 The One True Spirit Speaking…And a Body Thou hast Prepared for Me. Hebrews 10:5, Why Did God Need a Body of Flesh? For the reason that a Spirit cannot Shed Blood, Thus, The Birth of Jesus Christ, For God so loved the world He gave his only Begotten Son, The Only Fleshly body of GOD, In 2cd Corinthians 5:19, For God was In Christ Reconciling the World unto Himself, Singular}.

We find in 1st. Corinthians' 15:21 "For since by Man came Death, {Adam}By the Man Jesus Christ came Also the Resurrection of the Dead.

In 1st. Corinthians' 15:32 The Apostle Paul States, "If after the manner of Men I have Fought with "Beast" at Ephesus, what advantaged it me If the Dead rise not? Let us Eat and Drink; for tomorrow we all Die.

Paul's Preaching was if we have no hope of a Bodily Resurrection, Then what's the use' We might as well all "Eat and Drink for tomorrow we all Die with no Hope of a Bodily Resurrection.

Chapter 2

Apostle Paul's Discussion with the Corinthians

Paul's earlier discussion with the Corinthians was if the Dead rise not, then I am a liar without Hope. Let us then eat and drink for tomorrow we all Die. However, the Apostle Paul continues to discuss with them saying' if there is no resurrection of the dead, then there is no necessity for a bodily change. Here I'm Thankful that I do not believe in Cremation of a Holy Ghost Filled Person and Their Body Being Burned to Ashes. Also, I'm Thankful God Did not allow the Romans /Jews to Cremate the Body of our Lord Jesus Christ. *God Had a Plan!*

Reading in 1st Corinthians chapter 15 verse 42, speaking of the resurrection of the dead body {not The Spirit} it 'the body, it is sown (Buried) in corruption, it, the Body is raised in incorruption: It the Body is sown in dishonor; it the Body is raised in Glory: it the Body is sown in weakness; it the Body is raised in Power: 1st Corinthians chapter 15 verse 44 reads; It is sown a Natural Body; it is raised a Body incorruptible and Immortal. There is a Natural Body (FLESH) and there is a

Spiritual Body. Jesus Christ was raised as a Spiritual Body, He was Raised Incorruptible and Immortal. when He was resurrected from the grave He Showed

Himself Alive 40 Days, Speaking to them the apostles of the things pertaining to the Kingdom of God.

In the book of Romans chapter 15 verse 45 The first man Adam was made a living Soul, a {Natural Body} The Last man Adam was made a quickening Spirit.

Chapter 3

Recapitulation

In the process of Recapitulation? when our Bodies meets our spirits to be rejoined in that Heavenly Host to be known in Heaven as we were known in the earth, Thus the Resurrection. Christ undoes the wrong that Adam did, Jesus now leads humanity to eternal life with God.

Read Romans chapter 8 verse 11...If that same SPIRIT that dwelt in Jesus Christ dwells in you, it shall also QUICKEN, a Verb, to make alive, to stimulate, to stir up faster, to Quicken your Mortal Body. research the word Quicken, to stir up, Make Alive, to meet him in the Air.

A spiritual Body does not mean an Invisible Body that cannot be touched or seen, but simply a body that has been changed from Mortal to Immortality.

Jesus after the Resurrection, appearing in the upper room, said to them; Handle Me and See It Is I, A Spirit has not Flesh and Bone as you see me have. He was in His changed Bloodless Body, a Tangible Touchable Body. Gods Purpose is to Sum up all things In Christ. Ephesians, chapter 1verse 10... in the

DISPENSATION of the Fullness of Time, He might gather together in ONE ALL things in Christ, which or in Heaven and which or on Earth, Even in Him. That Scripture declares the end of what we know as TIME. Yes, He is Coming, and we shall ALL be caught up together to meet him whether be awake or Asleep {Dead} All Shall be Changed, Thus, A Resurrection of both alive and dead.

In 1st Thessalonians Chapter 4 verse 16 Apostle Paul Declares' "For the Lord Himself shall descend from heaven with a Shout and the Voice of the Arch Angel, and with the Trump of God: And the Dead in Christ shall rise First: Thus, Again Reinforcing the Recapitulation. Again, emphasizing the importance of Ephesians 1:10, THAT in the dispensation of the fullness of Time (Time shall Be No More) He the Lord Jesus Christ shall Gather together All things IN Christ, Both which or in Heaven and which or on Earth, Even in Him. And we know the only way to be in him' Christ, is to be Baptized into Christ. The Lord tells us to Occupy till He Comes. In 1st Thessalonians Chapter 5 verse 1 But the Times and the Seasons brethren, you have no need I write unto you. For yourselves know perfectly that the Day of the Lord so cometh as a Thief in the night. 1st Thessalonians, verse 6, Therefore let us not sleep as do others but let us watch and be sober. For if we believe that Jesus Died and Rose again, {RESURRECTED} even so them also which sleep in Jesus will God Bring with Him. For this we say by the word of the Lord,

That we which are Alive and Remain unto the coming of the Lord shall not Prevent them which or Asleep.

Chapter 4

Apostle Paul's Second discussion with the Corinthians

A body that has been changed from Corruption to Incorruption, Is However still Tangible, Touchable, still visible Flesh. In comparison the same Body that went to the cross, that came forth from the grave, entered that room where the eleven disciples were sitting.

Read for Yourself in Luke chapter 24 verse 36...Jesus "HIMSELF" stood in the midst of them, and said unto them, Peace be unto you. In Verse 37...But they were terrified and Affrighted, and supposed they had seen a spirit, a Ghost:

In Luke 24:39.... He Said' Behold my hands and my feet, that it is I MYSELF: Handle ME and see, for a Spirit hath not Flesh and Bone as you see ME Have. Remember this is a Miracle, there is no Blood in his body, It stayed on the ground at Calvary. This Body, This same Jesus,

This very Example, is the glorious future of every Born Again, Person Baptized in Jesus Name and Filled with The Holy Ghost. His Victory over Death, hell, and the Grave, is what gives us our Hope while living in our earthly Natural Bodies. It is the hope of a Resurrected Body as Jesus has Portrayed it' Your Body, will be Fashioned after his, Jesus Christ's own Body, A Glorious Body.

God showed Job this Mystery in Christ the Hope of Glory. before the Birth of Jesus Christ, In Job chapter 14 verse 7-14. Job declares, For there is Hope of a tree if it be cut down, that it will sprout again, and the tender branch thereof will not cease. Though the Root thereof wax old in the earth, and the stock thereof die in the Ground, yet at the scent of water it will bud and bring forth boughs like a plant. But Man, Lieth down and wasteth away, yea man gives up the ghost, and where is he?

Verse 12 quotes' So man lieth down and RISETH not TILL the heavens be no more, (Remember Ephesians 1:10) They shall not awake or be Raised out of their sleep.

Oh, that thou would hide me in the grave, that thou would keep me Secret, until thy wrath be past, that thou appoint me a set time and remember Me!

If a man dies, shall he live again? All the days of my appointed time, will I wait till my CHANGE comes? Even today, Job is still waiting for his change to come, At The coming of our Lord and Savior Jesus Christ. Job Chapter 19 vs. 25-27 For I know that my Redeemer liveth, and he shall stand at the latter day (Ephesian's 1:10) upon the earth: And though after my Skin worms destroy this body, yet in my FLESH shall I See God: Whom I shall see for myself, and mine eyes shall behold, and not Another, though my reins be consumed within me. Jobs Hope continues till today and so is the hope of every Born-Again Believer.

Chapter 5

The Key

Most people will argue with you and the Scripture That they or ready for the coming of the Lord.

I hear it every day, I have accepted the Lord Jesus Christ As my Personal Savior, and that's fine but to be in the Bride of Christ you will First have to obey the gospel as Jesus Christ Instructed to Nicodemus in John chapter 3 verse 3…I say unto thee, except a Man be Born again He cannot see the Kingdom of God. Nicodemus saith unto Jesus, how can a man be born when he is old? Can he enter the second time into his mother's womb, and be born? Jesus said, Verily, Verily, I say unto thee, Except a Man be born of Water and of THE Spirit, He cannot enter Into the Kingdom of God. Notice the emphasis was not put on Water He was saying Any water will Do, as long as it is enough to be a Watery Grave.

River water, Creek Water, Lake Water, Swimming pool water, Bathtub water Even Cow Tub Water, Many Churches have Baptized in an 8 ft by 3ft water trough, as long as you can submerge the whole body, The Baptizer must (BURY) the old man. This is a conscious act of cleanliness,

Christening a body by pouring water on your head Does not bury you. Jesus said Born of the Water not sprinkled with it. However,

He did emphasize THE SPRIT, because there is only ONE, Deuteronomy Chapter 6 verse 4, Hear, O Israel: The LORD our GOD Is ONE LORD: John, 14 vs. 6, Jesus saith unto Philip, I am The Way the Truth and the Life: No Man cometh unto the father, But by me. John 14, Vs.7 Thomas, If Ye had known me, you should have known my Father Also: and from henceforth ye know Him and have SEEN Him.

Ephesians 4, 4, There is One Body, and One Spirit as ye or called in One Hope. Ephesians 4, Vs. 5, One Lord, One Faith, One Baptism.

Chapter 6

Apostle Paul's Third Discussion with the Corinthians

The Apostle Paul describes a Mystery in first Corinthians. Now everybody likes a good Mystery.

In 1st Corinthians 15 verse 51. Paul quotes' Behold I Show you a Mystery; We shall not all sleep, but we shall all be "CHANGED", {wowowo I LOVE THIS}, In a moment, in the twinkling of an eye, at the last trump, Revelation 10 verse 7, The Mystery of God Shall be Finished. Along with 1st Thessalonians chapter 4 verse 16, for the trumpet shall sound, Which Trumpet, yep you are right, the Last Trumpet, and the Dead shall be raised Incorruptible and "WE"

Our natural bodies shall be changed. 1st Corinthians Verse 54 … So, when this corruptible shall put on incorruption and this "MORTAL" shall have put on Immortality, then shall be brought to pass the saying' O Death where is thy sting? O Grave where is thy Victory.

Death and the Grave are not for Spirits, you don't bury spirits you bury Dead Bodies, that will come forth in the power of the Resurrection.

You can read about the Seventh Trumpet and the Mystery of God when it is finished in the 10th chapter of Revelations verse 7.

Revelation 10:7 goes along with Ephesians Chapter 1 verse 10...That in the dispensation of the fullness of times He {The Lord Jesus Christ} might gather together in one, all things in Christ. 'Better get Ready.

Jesus Declared in Revelation 1:18...I am He that Liveth and was Dead; and behold I am alive

for evermore, A-men; and have the Keys of hell and of Death. I realize I Reiterate a Lot of Scripture, I do because I want you the reader to Know the Importance of this great Event to take place in our Lives.

HOLD ON JESUS IS COMING!

Reiteration; Ephesians 1:10 That in the dispensation of the fullness of Time (Time shall Be No More) He the Lord Jesus Christ shall Gather together All things IN Christ, Both which or in Heaven and which or on Earth, Even in Him.

And we know the only way to be in Christ is to be Baptized into Christ. The Lord tells us to Occupy till He Comes. 1 Thessalonians Chapter 5 Vs. 1 But the Times and the Seasons, brethren, you have no need I write unto you. For yourselves know perfectly that the Day of the Lord so cometh as a Thief in the night. Verse 6, Therefore let us not sleep as do others but let us watch and be sober.

For if we believe that Jesus Died and Rose again, even so them also which sleep in Jesus will God Bring with Him. For this we say by the word of the Lord, that we which are Alive and Remain unto the coming of the Lord shall not Prevent them which or Asleep.

CHAPTER 7

THE PROPHECIES OF JOB

Reiteration; Job types the physical Body to that of a tree. In Job chapter 14:7…For there is hope of a tree, if it be cut down, that it will sprout again. Verse 8… Though the root thereof waxes old in the earth, and the stock thereof dies in the ground; yet through the scent of water it will bud, and bring forth boughs like a plant.

Wow! What a wonderful description of the tree typed like that of our Bodies, yes, we will die, yes, we will be buried in the ground, and yes, we through the scent of "LIVING WATER" shall live again.

Jesus is our Living Water. In John 4:10…Jesus Answered and said unto her If thou newest the gift of God and who it is that sayeth to thee, Give me to drink, thou would have asked of him and he would have given thee Living Water. Verse 14… But whosoever drinketh of the water that I shall give him, shall be in him a well springing up into Everlasting life.

In John chapter 7:37…On that last great day of the feast Jesus stood and cried if any man thirst let Him come unto me and drink. He that Believeth on me as the scriptures has said, out of his belly shall flow Rivers of Living Water.

I ask you, how much greater are you than The root or the stock of a Tree?

THE Reiterated KEY

Most people will argue with you and the ScriptureThat they or ready for the coming of the Lord. I hear it every day, I have accepted the Lord Jesus Christ As my Personal Savior, and that's fine but to be in the Bride of Christ you will First have to obey the gospel as Jesus Christ Instructed to Nicodemus in John chapter 3 verse 3…I say unto thee, except a Man be Born again He cannot see the Kingdom of God. Nicodemus saith unto Jesus, how can a man be born when he is old? Can he enter the second time into his mother's womb, and be born? Jesus said, Verily, Verily, I say unto thee, Except a Man be born of Water and of THE Spirit, He cannot enter Into the Kingdom of God. Notice the emphasis was not put on Water He was saying Any water will Do, enough to be a Watery Grave, River water, Creek Water, Lake Water, Swimming pool water, Bathtub water As long as you can submerge the whole body, The Baptizer must (BURY) the old man. This is a conscious act of cleanliness, Christening a body Does not bury it. Jesus said Born of Water not sprinkled with it. However, He did emphasize THE SPRIT, Because there is only ONE, Deuteronomy Chapter 6 verse 4, Hear, O Israel: The LORD our GOD Is ONE LORD: John, 14 vs. 6, Jesus saith unto Philip, I am The Way the Truth and the Life: No Man cometh unto the father, But by me. Vs.7 If Ye had known me, you should have known my Father Also: and from henceforth ye know Him and have Seen Him. Ephesians 4, 4 There is One Body, and One Spirit as ye or called in One Hope. Vs. 5 One Lord, One Faith, One Baptism.

Chapter 8

The Prophecies of Job Continued

God gave Job a revelation like no other concerning the Resurrection of the Body. So, we go to the book of Job Chapter 14:12...So Man lieth down and riseth not: Till the Heavens be no more, they shall not awake nor be raised out of their sleep until the voice of the 7th angel: Rev.10:7 And the Dispensation of Time is Over Ephesians 1:10.

In Job 14:13...O that thou wouldest hide me in the GRAVE, that thou wouldest keep me secret, until thy wrath be past, that thou wouldest appoint me a set time, and Remember Me.

Job's Hope, in Chap.14: Vs.14...If a Man Die, Shall He Live again? All the days of my appointed time, will I wait till my "CHANGE" come.

What about that my friend, what are you waiting for. Job was not referring to Pocket CHANGE, He was waiting for the great Catching Away when that 7th Trumpet Sounds.

Job Chap, 14 In Vs, 25 Job quotes...For I Know my Redeemer Liveth, {JESUS CHRIST} And that He shall stand at the Latter Day upon the Earth: And Though after my Skin Worms destroy my Body, Yet in my FLESH shall "I" See GOD: Whom I shall See for myself, And Mine Eyes shall Behold, And not Another.

Though my reins be consumed within Me. "That sounds Personal to me". Job Had the Revelation of the Change to come' Mortal to Immortality, From Corruption to Incorruption

Believers and Patriarchs

How Beautiful foretold, the prophecies describing the Bodily Resurrection. Job was already dead and in the ground when the Lord Jesus Christ Resurrected His Own Body from the Grave. I feel like every Old Testament "faith Saint" had a hope or feeling of something better.

Romans 4:13...For the Promise that He should be the Heir of the world was not to Abraham or to his Seed through the Law...But only through the Righteousness of Faith.

In the book of Romans chapter four verse twenty we read about the Hope of Abraham...He Staggered not at the promises of God through un belief; but was strong in Faith giving Glory to God: Romans 4:23...Now it was not written for his sake alone, that it was imputed to him; but for us also, to whom it shall be imputed if we believe on Him That raised up Jesus our Lord from the Dead, who was delivered for our offenses and was Raised again for our Justification.

In Romans 11:10...For He "Abraham" looked For a city which hath foundations, whose builder and maker is God. Romans 4:39 Speaking of all the Patriarchs that believed, and all these having obtained a good report through faith Received not the Promise: God having provided some better thing for us, that they, The Old time Saints and Patriarchs without us, should not be made perfect.

23

Chapter 9

Paul's Discussion with the Romans

In Chapter eight of the book of Romans the Apostle Paul Emphasizes the facts, That a person must be Born of the Spirit. The reason for that fact is, That the Power of the Resurrection is only to the Believer that has been Born again of the "Water" Baptized, John 3: Vs 5, Totally Submerged With the officiator pronouncing the Baptism to be In The Name of Jesus Christ for the Remission of Sins and then being Born of the Spirit "the Holy Ghost" with the Evidence of Speaking in Other Tongues Acts 2:4 As the Sprit gives Utterance.

Paul clearly announced in Romans 8:9...Now if Any Man have NOT the Spirit of Christ, He is none of His. Verse 11 declares, But if the Spirit of him that raised up Jesus from the dead dwell in you, He that raised up Christ from the dead shall also Quicken (Raise) your Mortal Body, by the same Spirit that dwelleth in you, not your Mortal Spirit, but your Mortal Body.

In verse 18 Paul states; for I reckon that the Sufferings of this present time or not worthy to be compared with the

Glory which shall be revealed in us. For the Earnest expectation of the creature Waiteth for the Manifestation of the sons of God.

For the Creature {first man Adam} was made subject to vanity, not willingly, but by reason of him who has subjected the same {Creature} Us, in Hope.

Because the creature itself {The Body} also shall be delivered from the bondage of Corruption into the Glorious Liberty of the Children of God.

Paul's Discussion with the Romans Continued

Romans 8:22...For we know that the whole creation Groaned and travailed in Pain together Until now. And not only they, but ourselves also Which have the first fruits of the Spirit, (first receivers of the HOLY GHOST Acts 2:38, even we, within ourselves waiting for the Adoption to wit, The Redemption of our BODIES.

Note: About the above scripture it has been said by some that 'Adoption' only Means to become adopted into the family of God.

Well, In the first place we are certainly not adopted into the family of God, but rather we or Born Again into the Family of God 'read John 3: 3,5. The Teaching to Nicodemus. Jesus said Flesh and Blood cannot enter the Kingdom of God. However, My Friend, Immortal Flesh and Bone can and is Redeemed into the Kingdom. When Jesus entered into the upper room he was Flesh and Bone. The Blood that gives us Mortal life was not in his Body it was in the Ground at the foot of the cross, Luke 24:36

Likewise, you and I will be changed from the Mortal Body of flesh and blood to the immortal body of Glorified Flesh and Bone. This is the Hope of every Man that Believeth.

The Scriptures Declare in 1st. John 3:2...It doth not yet appear what we shall be, but we know when he shall appear, we shall be like him for we shall see him as he is. I again ask you a question my friend, How Is HE?

The Same Subjected Unto Hope

The Answer to the Question of How IS HE Is in Acts 1:9,11...He is Immortal, Incorruptible, Visible, Tangible, and while being received into Glory two Men, Angels: stood by them The Apostles and brethren, Two Men in white apparel, which also said, Ye Men of Galilee, why stand ye gazing up into Heaven? This SAME Jesus which is taken up from you into Heaven "Shall So Come in Like Manner" as ye have seen him go into Heaven.

And The Apostle Paul to the Thessalonians, 1st Thess. 4:13...I would not have you to be Ignorant Brethren, concerning them which are asleep, that Ye sorrow not even as others that have NO Hope.

For if we Believe that Jesus Died and Rose again, even so them which also sleep in Jesus will God bring with Him. In 1st. Thessalonian's. Verse 16...For the Lord Himself {Remember the Angels Promise in Acts 1: 11, This Same Jesus} shall descend from Heaven with a shout, with the voice of the Archangel, and with the trump of God {Remember Rev.10:7 At the Last Trump} And the Dead {Not the Spirit} In Christ shall rise First. Why does the dead in Christ rise First?

Because their Hope was pre-Subjected, hope they have never seen, but hope they looked for, These are they which follow the lamb where so ever he goeth. These are they that have obeyed the gospel, 1. Repented of their Sins, 2. Were Baptized in The Name Jesus Christ for the Remission of those sins and filled with his Holy Ghost. They or The Lambs Bride, written in the Lambs Book of Life, Rev. 20:12. Remember, The Dead shall be judged out of the 66 books of the Bible, But the Bride of Christ those that were Baptized into Christ, weather they or asleep or alive Their Names or Written in the Lambs Book of Life Prejudged Not by the 66 books, but by the Lambs Book of life.

An Order of Events

Remember the DEAD in Christ shall rise First. Then we which are alive and remain shall be caught up together with them. Abraham never saw that city the New Jerusalem, yet he looked for it in hope, He will see it, He will be made perfect or changed, but not until the Bride of Jesus Christ in the Ground Rise First, Thessalonians 4;15-16 For We which are Alive and Remain Shall not be caught up without Them. Hebrews 11:40…God having provided some better thing for us, that they {Abraham, the Patriarchs, the Faith Saints} Without us {The Jesus Name Bride}Should not be made perfect. Even in the Resurrection there is an order of events.

In 1st Cor. 15:23…But every man in his own order: Christ's the First Fruits; afterward they that are Christ's at his coming, then cometh the end.

I expressed my opinion concerning what it takes to be in the Bride of Christ. To be in the Bride of Christ you must repent, acts 2:38...A type of Death, Dying to this world of Sin. You must be Baptized, (Buried) Acts 2:38 into the Name of Jesus Christ for the remission of sins, Galatians 3:27, For as many of you as have been Baptized Into Christ have put on Christ. And Romans 6:2...Know ye not that so many of us that were Baptized into Christ were Baptized into His Death; You must be buried with Christ to be Resurrected with Him. And only through the Burial Process in water in The Name above every name, Acts 4:12, Jesus Name, Note' that the Blood is in the Water. It is the only time the Blood is Applied, In the Water and the sins of your Body or remitted. Matthew 19:34 But one of the soldiers with a spear Pierced His side, and forthwith came there out Both Blood and Water. These or Synonymous they come together. You cannot receive one without the other, It's in the water. There or three that bear witness in the Earth, The Spirit, The Water and The Blood: 1st John Chapter 5 Verse 7. and these Three Agree in one, They or conjoined together in One Body That of the Lord Jesus Christ. And you my Friend can receive all three when you obey the scripture in Acts Chapter 2 verse 38. John 5:11, and this is the Record, that God has given to us Eternal Life, And this Life is in His Son.

The Conclusion of Proof and Facts

In closing I want to leave other scriptures for you to study. The Scripture teaches us in 2cd Tim. 2:15... Study to show thyself approved unto God A workman that needeth not to be ashamed, rightly dividing the word of Truth.

Many Scriptures will lead you to the Applications of truth. To examine for yourselves and be fully persuaded in your own mind, what is that perfectly and acceptable will of God in your Life.

See Acts 2:4,38 - Acts 4:12 - Acts 8:20 Acts 10:36 - Acts 19:2 -1st. Cor. 10:1,2 Phil. 2:10 - Colossians 3:1 - Rev. 10 - Rev. 22

It is the writers Prayer that the reader of this Word would carefully search his heart and mind in the peace of God. This Subject has been often attacked by those that oppose the Resurrection of a Natural Body Doctrine in the Word of God.

This Subject is not intended for offense or gainsay merely an announcement of Truth backed up by the scriptures in the word of God, to bring truth to the forefront. To Strengthen

and unite The Brethren in the Faith, that was once delivered
unto the Saints.

God Bless you all,
Sincerely, in His Service.

Elder, Roland RJ Buras

www.ingramcontent.com/pod-product-compliance
Lightning Source LLC
Chambersburg PA
CBHW072142150726
48002CB00004B/1593